MATH
PUZZLES
FOR THE CLEVER MIND

D0167714

MATH
PUZZLES
FOR THE CLEVER MIND

DERRICK NIEDERMAN

PUZZLE
WRIGHT
PRESS

New York

PUZZLE WRIGHT PRESS

New York

An Imprint of Sterling Publishing
387 Park Avenue South
New York, NY 10016

PUZZLEWRIGHT PRESS and the distinctive Puzzlewright Press logo are registered trademarks of Sterling Publishing Co., Inc.

© 2001 by Derrick Niederman

First Puzzlewright Press edition published in 2013.

All rights reserved. No part of this publication may be reproduced, stored in a retrieval system, or transmitted, in any form or by any means, electronic, mechanical, photocopying, recording, or otherwise, without prior written permission from the publisher.

ISBN 978-1-4549-0973-6

Distributed in Canada by Sterling Publishing
℅ Canadian Manda Group, 165 Dufferin Street
Toronto, Ontario, Canada M6K 3H6
Distributed in the United Kingdom by GMC Distribution Services
Castle Place, 166 High Street, Lewes, East Sussex, England BN7 1XU
Distributed in Australia by Capricorn Link (Australia) Pty. Ltd.
P.O. Box 704, Windsor, NSW 2756, Australia

For information about custom editions, special sales, and premium and corporate purchases, please contact Sterling Special Sales at 800-805-5489 or specialsales@sterlingpublishing.com.

Manufactured in the United States of America

2 4 6 8 10 9 7 5 3 1

www.puzzlewright.com

Contents

Introduction

Some books make for wonderful bedside reading. *Math Puzzles for the Clever Mind* isn't one of them. Once you start reading, you'll be challenged, prodded, and, who knows, maybe even fooled. But it's all in the spirit of fun. It was your clever mind that caused you to pick up this book, and I certainly want to give it a workout.

The puzzles inside are a combination of new ideas, personal favorites, and classic puzzles to which I've added just a little bit extra. Some have surprise answers, but none involves higher mathematics. You already have all the tools you need. My only disappointment is that I now know all the answers, and I can't do the puzzles myself!

If you like what's inside, at least I'll sleep at night. But don't thank just me. My editor Peter Gordon is quite a puzzle person himself, as is Fraser Simpson, who made some crucial suggestions down the stretch.

Enjoy!

—Derrick Niederman

Puzzles

I. LAZY DAYS OF SUMMER

The digits 1, 2, 3, and 4 can be arranged to form 24 different four-digit numbers. What is the sum of those 24 numbers? (There is a shortcut, in case you don't want to write them all down and add them all up!)

2. PIECES OF EIGHT

Suppose a wooden cube measures eight units on a side. If you cut the cube into eight identical smaller cubes, how long is a side of one of the smaller cubes?

3. SOMETHING IS MISSING

In the array of numbers below, what number should go where the question mark is?

3	11	21	41	91
6	14	15	23	53
3	5	6	8	?

4. SEEING SPOTS

A regular six-faced die has 21 spots altogether. Without looking at any dice you might have lying around, how many of these spots are in the center of one of the faces? How many are at one corner or another? How many are somewhere else?

5. FILL IN THE BLANKS

Fill in each box below with one of +, −, ×, or ÷ to produce a valid equation:

$$12 \; \square \; 2 \; \square \; 7 \; \square \; 4 = 9$$

6. HOW FAR?

The number 907 is prime: it has no factors other than itself and 1. To prove that 907 is prime, you must check to see that it is not divisible by any prime number, beginning with 2, 3, 5, and so on. The question is, how far do you need to go before you can conclude that 907 is in fact prime?

7. MARY, QUITE CONTRARY

When you were growing up, there was a girl named Mary in your neighborhood. All you remember about Mary is that 1) she knew she wanted to live in New York City when she grew up, 2) she had her sights on becoming a doctor, and 3) she organized a bowling party for her 16th birthday. Given all this, which of the following statements is most likely to be true about Mary today?

- A) Mary is a doctor who lives in New York City and goes bowling on Tuesdays.
- B) Mary lives in New York City and goes bowling on Tuesdays.
- C) Mary goes bowling on Tuesdays.

8. ON ALL FOURS

What is the smallest whole number that, when multiplied by 3, gives an answer consisting of all 4's?

9. GAME OF THE CENTURY

Two players play a game that begins with Player A calling out a number between 1 and 10. Player B then calls out another number; B's number must be bigger than A's, but it cannot exceed A's number by more than 10. (In other words, if Player A calls out "6," Player B cannot call out "17" or higher.) The players continue in this fashion. The winner of the game is the player who calls out the number 100.

Which player can always win the game, A or B?

10. DON'T LEAVE ME OUT

The junior high school basketball team consists of just seven kids. From that group of seven, it is possible to create 21 different starting teams of five players. Suppose one of the team members is named Jerry. How many of the 21 possible starting teams include Jerry?

11. SO FAR, YET SO CLOSE

By adding just one line to the equation below, form a *correct* equation. And in case you were wondering, you cannot use the line to convert the equals sign into an inequality!

$$5+5+5=550$$

12. DOUBLY TRUE

The equations below are already true, provided you understand the languages involved. The first one, in Roman numerals, means 51 + 51 = 102. The second one, in Spanish, means that 2 + 2 + 3 = 7.

By replacing each letter with a number, can you make the resulting numerical equations also true?

The standard rules are as follows: 1) Once a number is substituted for a letter it must stand for each appearance of that letter, 2) different letters must be assigned different numbers, and 3) none of the leftmost digits are zero.

$$
\begin{array}{cc}
 & L \ I \\
+ & L \ I \\
\hline
C & I \ I \\
\end{array}
$$

$$
\begin{array}{cccc}
 & D & O & S \\
 & D & O & S \\
+ & T & R & E & S \\
\hline
S & I & E & T & E \\
\end{array}
$$

13. WAGERING ABOVEBOARD

Two men play some games of chess for the stakes of one dollar per game. (This means that each player puts in a dollar and the winner of the game receives both dollars.) When the games are completed, the first man has won three games and the second has won three dollars. Assuming that none of the games ended in a draw, how many games did they play?

14. RUN-ON SENTENCE

Insert digits into the blanks in the box below to make true statements. For example, you can't put a 1 in the second blank because then that statement would read that the number of 1's in the box is 1, when in fact the two 1's on that line would be two occurrences of the digit 1. The solution is unique.

The number of 0's in this box is ___.

The number of 1's in this box is ___.

The number of 2's in this box is ___.

The number of 3's in this box is ___.

The number of 4's in this box is ___.

The number of 5's in this box is ___.

The number of 6's in this box is ___.

The number of 7's in this box is ___.

The number of 8's in this box is ___.

The number of 9's in this box is ___.

15. DIVIDING LINE

The town of Braddock is one mile north and one mile east of Alton. Clancy is eight miles due east of Braddock. Consider the triangle formed by drawing segments joining the three towns. If you draw a line from north to south that cuts this triangle into two pieces of equal area, how far is this line from Braddock?

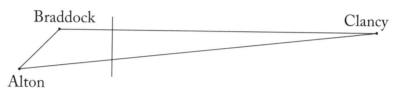

16. TEACHERS' SPAT

The ten digits are divided into two groups as follows:

$$1 \quad 4 \quad 7$$

$$0 \quad 2 \quad 3 \quad 5 \quad 6 \quad 8 \quad 9$$

A math teacher and an art teacher were shown this arrangement, and each was asked to explain the rule that created the two groups. "Why, that's obvious," the math teacher exclaimed. Meanwhile, the art teacher announced, "I got it immediately." Yet the two teachers had entirely different rules in mind. What were they?

17. HEAD START

Chris and Jean play a game of flipping a coin. It's a simple game—the first person to flip a "heads" wins! If Chris goes first and the two alternate flips after that, what is the probability that Chris will win the game?

18. PLAYING THE TRIANGLE

An isosceles triangle is a triangle in which two of the sides have the same length. Suppose you have a triangle and you know that two of the sides have lengths 17 and 8. If that triangle is isosceles, how long is the third side?

19. TAKING THE NINTH

An enterprising student calculated the ninth powers of the numbers 21, 22, 23, and so on, all the way to the ninth power of 29. Unfortunately, her paper was torn, and all she had left were the last six digits of all these numbers. Worse still, they weren't even in order!

However, she was still able to identify which of the ninth powers belonged with which of the original numbers from 21 to 29—without doing the calculations all over again. Can you do the same? (It's easier than it looks!)

$$...484987$$
$$...661463$$
$$...975869$$
$$...265625$$
$$...540224$$
$$...046581$$
$$...953408$$
$$...217792$$
$$...678976$$

20. AVERAGES MADE EASY

Can you come up with whole numbers A and B such that $(A + B)/2 = A.B$? (That's a decimal point between the A and B.)

If A and B both equal zero, the equation works, but the idea is to come up with non-zero solutions. It might help to know that there are infinitely many solutions.

21. SIZES AND SHAPES

In the figure below, an equilateral triangle has been wedged in between two circles. How does the diameter of the smaller circle compare to the diameter of the larger circle?

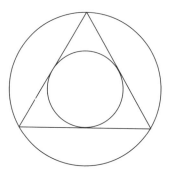

22. MY THREE SONS

A man has three sons. The oldest is three years older than the middle son, and the middle son is three years older than the youngest. Altogether, the three sons' ages add up to 57. How old are the three sons?

23. WATER UNDER THE BRIDGE

Four men have to cross a deep ravine at night. There is a bridge across the ravine, but it is old and rickety and can only support the weight of two men at a time. They have one flashlight to use among them, and since they need the light to see their way across, if two men cross at the same time, they must travel at the speed of the slower man. The fastest man of the group takes one minute to cross the bridge, the next fastest takes two minutes, the third fastest takes five minutes, and the slowest man takes a full 10 minutes to cross the bridge.

What is the shortest amount of time in which all four

men can get across the ravine? Don't forget that the men need the flashlight to see their way across, so someone must bring the flashlight back if there's anyone left to cross the bridge. (Hint: The answer is less than 19 minutes!)

24. LUCKY 13

The diagram you see consists of seven line segments and six circles. Place the numbers 1 through 13 on either a line or a circle in such a way that the number on each segment is the *difference* of the two numbers at its endpoints. There is more than one possible solution.

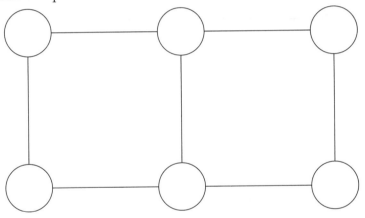

25. PRIME MOVERS

Although 18 is not a prime number, it can be made prime by changing a single digit—say the 8 to a 7. Similarly, 981 is not prime, but by changing the middle digit to a 1, we get the prime number 911.

What is the smallest number that cannot be made prime by changing a single digit?

26. A BURNING PROBLEM

Three wicks that are not attached to anything have the property that if you light one end of any of them, that wick will take exactly one hour to burn completely. But the rate of burning is not uniform, which makes the following problem a bit trickier than it might have been.

You are given these three lengths of wick together with a lighter. How can you measure a time interval of precisely one hour, 45 minutes with these three wicks?

27. SUM-DAY SOON

Some people believe that January 1, 2000 is the first day of the 21st century. Other people feel that the honor belongs to January 1, 2001. But everyone should agree that January 1, *2002* is the first "sum-day" of the new century—when you write out that date in standard notation it becomes 01/01/02, and 1 + 1 = 2. More generally, a sum-day is a date in which the day and month add up to the year. With that in mind,

A) What is the last sum-day of the 21st century?

B) How many sum-days are there in the 21st century?

28. CUBIC MEASURE

A giant wooden cube is painted green on all six sides and then cut into 125 identical, smaller cubes. How many of these smaller cubes are painted green on exactly two faces?

29. HOW NOW, BROWN COW?

A farmer owns several dairy cows, some black and some brown. He finds that 4 black cows and 3 brown cows give the same amount of milk in 5 days as 3 black cows and 5 brown cows give in 4 days.

Which gives more milk in a day, a black cow or a brown cow?

30. UNLIKELY RESULT

Which is most likely?
   A) Getting heads at least once from the flipping of two coins?
   B) Getting heads at least twice from the flipping of four coins?
   C) Getting heads at least three times from the flipping of six coins?
   D) Getting heads at least four times from the flipping of eight coins?

31. CLOSE, BUT NO CIGAR

Jurgen bragged to his friends that he had done 20 percent better than Ian on his math test. Ian's score was 80, so everyone concluded that Jurgen had gotten a perfect score of 100. Although Jurgen didn't lie, the truth was that Jurgen hadn't scored perfectly. What was his actual score?

32. THE KNIGHT'S TOUR

Below is a 3 × 4 mini chessboard, with a knight stationed in the middle square of the first column. Suppose the knight travels in such a way that it lands on each of the other 11 squares once and only once, coming to rest somewhere on the bottom row.

Which of the four squares in the bottom row will the knight end up on? (It turns out that there is only one possibility.)

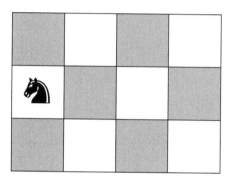

33. THE PICKY EATERS CLUB

There are 100 members of the picky eaters club. Only 15 of them have tried both cauliflower and spinach. Altogether, 72 of them have never tried cauliflower, and 81 have never tried spinach.

How many members of the picky eaters club have never tried cauliflower *or* spinach?

34. THE USUAL SUSPECTS

Four men are taken to police headquarters following a bank robbery. The police are certain that one of the men is guilty, but they don't know for sure which one did it. Here's what the four men had to say for themselves:

Alan: "Bill did it."

Bill: "Don did it."

Charlie: "I didn't do it."

Don: "Bill lied when he said I did it."

If only one of the four statements is true, who is the guilty man?

35. BORDERLINE CASE

What's the smallest number of colors required to fill in the map below? The only condition is that no two regions that border one another can be given the same color. (Regions that meet at a single point are not considered to be bordering one another.)

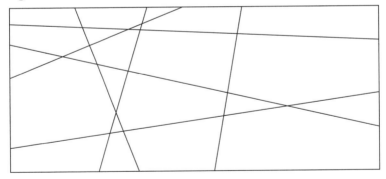

36. FILL IN THE BOXES

In the diagram below, place the numbers 1 through 42 into the boxes so that they form a continuous chain. In other words, starting with 1, you must be able to get to 2 by going left, right, up, or down (never diagonally), and so on, all the way to 42. Three numbers have already been placed for you.

	11	20				
	31					

37. PARENTHETICAL MENTION

By placing sets of parentheses in the proper places, make each of the following equations true:
   A) $2 + 2 \times 2 - 2 / 2 = 5$
   B) $2 + 2 \times 2 - 2 / 2 = 7$
   C) $2 + 2 \times 2 - 2 / 2 = 4$

38. NICKEL ARCADE

There is a simple game you might run into at amusement parks, fairs, or carnivals. The game consists of tossing a nickel onto a table marked something like the one below. The objective is to have the nickel come to rest *entirely* within one of the circles.

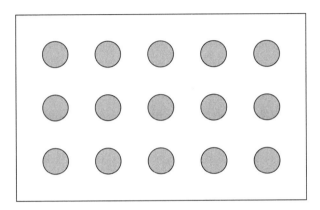

In real life the surface is bigger, of course. But suppose that each of the circles is two inches in diameter, that a nickel is one inch in diameter (it's smaller than that, actually), and that the distance between two adjacent circles is two inches, as is the distance between an outer circle and the edge of the table.

What do you suppose is the probability that you will win the game?

A) Over 20 percent

B) Between 10 and 20 percent

C) Less than 10 percent

39. EIGHT IS ENOUGH

Consider the following distribution of the first seven whole numbers:

| 1, 2, 4, 7 | | 3, 5, 6 |

Note that the sum of any two members of either box is either greater than the largest number (in this case, 7) or is in the other box.

Can you come up with an arrangement of the first *eight* whole numbers that satisfies the same two properties?

40. FIND THE SHORTCUT

We know that 5 cubed is $5 \times 5 \times 5 = 125$ and that 6 cubed is $6 \times 6 \times 6 = 216$. Suppose you are told that 148,877 is the cube of a whole number. What is that number?

(You don't need a calculator to do this problem. As with puzzle #19, once you find the right track, it's simpler than it first appears. It doesn't look simple, though, does it?)

41. MISSED ONE!

Of the ten decades that made up the 20th century, only one of them had no year that was divisible by 11. Which decade was that? (Here it is understood that a decade begins with the year ending in 0, so that the '20s consists of 1920 through 1929, and so on.)

42. THE MERRY-GO-ROUND

Place the numbers 1 through 9 in the nine circles of the merry-go-round below in such a way that the sum of any three circles on the same line is the same and is a multiple of 4. What number goes in the center circle?

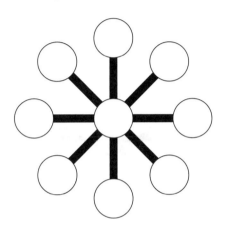

43. JUST FOR FUN

Can you anticipate the results of the following calculations?
A) $2^5 \times 9^2 = ?$
B) $6 + 6 + 6 + (6 \times 6 \times 6) + (6 \times 6 \times 6) + (6 \times 6 \times 6) = ?$
C) $12^2 + 33^2 = ?$
D) $(3 + 4 + 0 + 1 + 2 + 2 + 2 + 4)^6 = ?$
E) $4! + 0! + 5! + 8! + 5! = ?$
F) $3^3 + 4^4 + 3^3 + 5^5 = ?$

44. TARGET PRACTICE

In the target below, there are two black areas—the bull's-eye and the outermost ring—two white rings, and one gray ring. The radius of the bull's-eye is the same as the width of each of the outer rings. Show that the total white area equals the total black area.

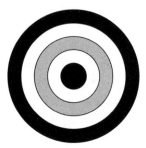

45. CANDY LAND

Three students have a box of candy they wish to share. Upon opening the first box, they count the number of candies inside and realize they can't share them equally. The same thing happens with the second box, although the second box contains 10 more candies than the first.

It turns out that the students can share the candies equally, provided they use *both* boxes. Why does this always work out?

46. ALL IN THE NEIGHBORHOOD

Sarah is a little baby, only 27 days old. But she's not even the youngest in her neighborhood. Little Melanie across the street is only three days old. Sarah is nine times as old as Melanie!

How many days will it be before Sarah is *four* times as old as Melanie?

47. MATCHSTICK MATCH

Imagine a square matchstick house set in a square matchstick yard, as in the diagram below. Your job is to place 10 matchsticks in the yard so that the yard is divided into five pieces of the same size and shape.

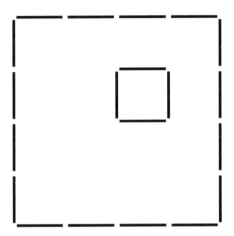

48. THROUGH THE LOOKING GLASS

Every once in a while a calendar year will be a palindrome, which means it reads the same way forward and backward. Starting with the year 10 A.D., can you come up with a pair of palindrome years that are

    A) 110 years apart?
    B) 11 years apart?
    C) 10 years apart?
    D) 2 years apart?

49. FULL OF HOT AIR

Three balloons—one red, one blue, and one yellow—escaped into the air. The combined height of the red and blue balloons was 140 meters. The combined height of the blue and yellow balloons was 135 meters. The combined height of the red and yellow balloons was 155 meters.

Which balloon was the highest of the three?

50. NIFTY FIFTY

Ben and Julie are playing a card game involving green and yellow cards. They get 3 points every time they draw a green card, and 5 points every time they draw a yellow card. The winner is the first one to reach 50 points.

Ben has 41 points now, and has 9 cards. How many cards does he have of each color?

51. TEN-LETTER DAY

Solve the following equation by substituting a digit (0, 1, 2, 3, 4, 5, 6, 7, 8, or 9) for each letter. As with all problems of this type, different letters must be given different digits. The three J's must be represented by the same digit. There is more than one possible solution.

$$
\begin{array}{r}
A\ B\ C \\
D\ E\ F \\
+\ G\ H\ I \\
\hline
J\ J\ J
\end{array}
$$

52. ODDS-ON FAVORITE

Three runners compete in a race. The probability that A will win is twice the probability that B will win. Similarly, the probability that B will win is twice the probability that C will win.

What is the precise probability that player A will win the race?

53. MAKING EVERYONE HAPPY

Mr. Townsend, the math teacher, knew he had his hands full when it came to parent conference day. Three sets of parents—the Abercrombies, Balderdashes, and Cockamamies—were all unusually competitive, and each had a child in Mr. Townsend's algebra class.

So when the Abercrombies came around, Mr. Townsend assured them that their child usually performed better on tests than the Balderdashes' child. He then turned around and told the Balderdashes that their child usually performed better on tests than the Cockamamies' child. And he told the Cockamamies that their child usually performed better on tests than the Abercrombies' child.

How is this possible?

54. ONE THROUGH NINE

Place a *different* digit in each of the nine blanks below so that each of the indicated equations is correct.

___ − ___ = ___

___ ÷ ___ = ___

___ + ___ = ___

55. SQUARE DEAL

It is easy to divide a square into four smaller squares. You simply draw two lines, one going up and down, the other going left to right, that cut the square in half.

It turns out to be impossible to divide a square into 2, 3, or 5 smaller squares, but all other subdivisions are possible. Can you find a way to divide a square into six smaller squares? How about seven smaller squares? The smaller squares are not all the same size.

56. LION IN WAITING

Here's one that has been circulated among puzzle diehards in recent years. Can you solve it?

Consider a closed-in pen containing 16 hungry lions and a single solitary sheep. If you are fearing for the sheep's life, your fears are well placed: all things being equal, any one of the lions would gladly eat the sheep.

Ah, but there is a snag. If any one of the lions devours the hapless sheep, that lion will become drowsy, and will become vulnerable to being eaten by another hungry lion. Any lion eating a lion gets drowsy, too.

In considering the fate of the solitary sheep, we are to assume that the best possible outcome for a lion would be to devour the sheep (or another lion) and thus satisfy his hunger; the next best outcome would be to remain hungry but remain alive; the worst outcome would be to eat the sheep (or another lion), only to be eaten in return. And we must also assume that the lions in question behave very, very logically.

Given all this, what happens to the sheep?

57. NO SQUARING REQUIRED

The triangle below is the famous 3-4-5 right triangle, "famous" because it satisfies the Pythagorean theorem: 3 squared plus 4 squared equals 5 squared.

As you can see, the 3-4-5 right triangle has been placed in a rectangle. What is the height of that rectangle? (You don't need the Pythagorean theorem to solve the problem!)

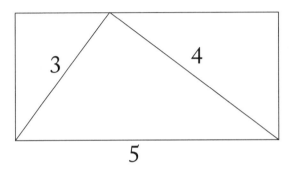

58. JUST FOR KICKS

In the game of American football, a touchdown (with one-point conversion) is worth 7 points, while a field goal is worth three points. What is the highest score that *cannot* be achieved by using a combination of converted touchdowns and field goals?

59. THE A&P

Can you come up with a rectangle whose sides are whole numbers and whose area (A) is numerically equal to its perimeter (P)? There are two solutions.

60. RADICAL MOVEMENT

Which has a greater value?

$$\sqrt{5\tfrac{5}{24}} \quad \text{or} \quad 5\sqrt{\tfrac{5}{24}}$$

61. DIVIDING LINES

One of the numbers 11,111 and 111,111 is a multiple of 11. Which one?

62. PROOF IN THE PUDDING

The Browns have three children: Mike, Sarah, and April. Mike said that he saw some pudding in the refrigerator and ate one-half of it. April said she saw some pudding in the refrigerator and ate one-third of it. Sarah said she saw some pudding in the refrigerator and ate all of it! It turns out that each of the three children had the same amount of pudding. What actually happened?

63. BOXING MATCH

Suppose that the two figures below are each folded up to form a box. Which box will fit more?

Note that the two diagrams are not drawn to scale!

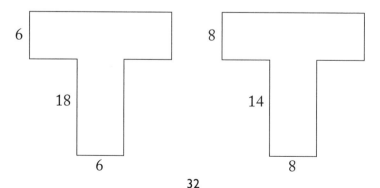

64. ODD QUESTION

How many odd three-digit numbers are there?

65. SIX-SHOOTER

Suppose n is a whole number. Can you explain why the number $n(n + 1)(2n + 1)$ must be divisible by 6?

Let's try a couple of examples. If we let $n = 3$, we get the value $3 \times 4 \times 7 = 84$. If $n = 8$, then we get $8 \times 9 \times 17 = 1224$. Both 84 and 1224 are divisible by 6. There are no exceptions. Your job is to figure out why!

66. LOOK BEFORE YOU LEAP

If each of the two dimensions of a rectangle is increased by 100%, by what percentage is the area increased?

67. BARNYARD COLLAGE

Many years ago, a farmer had 200 shekels with which to purchase 100 animals. Cows cost 20 shekels apiece, pigs cost 6 shekels apiece, while a sheep could be purchased for a single shekel. Assuming that he had to purchase at least one of each of the three animals, and assuming that he had to use all of his money, how many of each kind of animal did he purchase?

68. STRANGE SEQUENCE

What number completes the following eight-term sequence?

19   5   17   21   5   14   3   ?

69. SMALL BUT POWERFUL

What is the smallest integer greater than 1 that is both a perfect square and a perfect cube? What is the next smallest number to have the same property?

70. A BRIDGE TOO FAR

Two couples are enjoying a game of bridge. (Don't worry. You don't need to know how to play bridge in order to solve the puzzle. All you need to know is that four people play the game, and each player is dealt 13 cards.) Suppose that one couple—say, North-South—holds nine diamonds between them. Show that East-West must have at least eight cards in one of the other three suits.

71. BYE BYE BIRDIE

Fifty-seven players enter a badminton tournament. In order to even out the draw, a number of first-round byes are given out. A bye is defined as a free pass from the first round into the second round. The idea, as with any single-elimination tournament, is that the second-round participants then pair up, the winners of those matches pair up, and so on, until the tournament produces a single champion.

In order for the tournament to work properly, how many byes must be given out?

72. BE PERFECTLY FRANK

A hot dog vendor at a soccer game sells one-half of his supply of hot dogs during the first half of the game. During the intermission he sells a total of five hot dogs. During the second half he sells three-eighths of his original supply. He is left with only four hot dogs. How many did he have to start with?

73. THE CHRISTMAS CYCLE

Consider the various gifts in the song "The Twelve Days of Christmas." The first day's gift was the famous partridge in a pear tree; the second day's gifts included two turtle doves as well as the partridge; the third day featured three French hens in addition to the two turtle doves and the partridge, and so on, right up through the 12 drummers drumming.

Suppose that our house isn't big enough to fit all of our presents. If we had to give up one gift per day beginning the day after Christmas, how long would it be before we ran out of gifts?

74. SIX-POINT LANDING

Consider the set of six points below:

Connect nine pairs of these points with line segments in such a way that no three of the points form the vertices of a triangle.

75. CUT AND PASTE

Using two straight cuts, divide the region below into three pieces that can be reassembled to form a square.

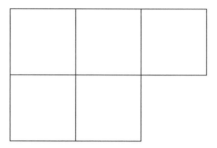

76. FRACTIONS OF THE WHOLE

The year 1972 was eventful. Mark Spitz won seven gold medals at the Summer Olympics in Munich, Germany. Bobby Fischer defeated Boris Spassky for the world chess championship, held in Reykjavik, Iceland. Meanwhile, back in the U.S.A., the author of this book graduated from high school!

Enough history. Can you express the fraction $19/72$ in the form $1/a + 1/b$, where a and b are whole numbers?

77. STRANGE RELATIONS

In the rectangle below, the numbers in the second row relate in some way to the numbers directly above them in the first row. If all of the numbers are whole numbers, what number goes in the box with the question mark?

12	6	3
6	3	?

78. DIGITAL PUBLISHING

A certain book has page numbers on every page. It turns out that if you count up all the digits of all the page numbers in the book, you get a total of exactly 300 digits. (For example, a 10-page book has a total of 11 digits in all the page numbers—nine for pages 1 through 9, and two for page 10.)

How many page numbers are in the book?

79. LETTER PERFECT

In the addition problem below, what number must be substituted for the letter A to make the addition work?

$$
\begin{array}{r}
A\ B \\
+\ B\ A \\
\hline
C\ A\ C
\end{array}
$$

80. CONNECT THE DOTS

Below are five dots. How many lines must be drawn in order to connect every dot with every other one?

•

•   •

•   •

81. MINDING YOUR P'S AND Q'S

Consider the system of equations below:

$$6249p + 3751q = 26{,}249$$
$$3751p + 6249q = 23{,}751$$

It looks pretty hard, doesn't it? It just so happens that there is only one pair of numbers p and q that satisfies both equations. In general, you need to use algebra to solve problems such as these. But the solution to this one is easier than you might think, provided you find the shortcut. Care to give it a try?

82. MAKING THE GRADE

A class of fewer than 30 students took a test. The results were mixed. One-third of the class received a "B," one-fourth received a "C," one-sixth received a "D," and one-eighth of the class flunked. Everyone else got an "A."

How many students in the class got an "A" on the test?

83. FEEDING THE SQUARE ROWS

In the six rows of numbers below, each of the pairs adds up to 25. Now, 25 happens to be a perfect square. Can you fill in the blanks with a third number—a different number for each row—so that the sum of *any* two numbers on *any* row is a perfect square? (There is a definite pattern to the answers!)

$$1, 24, \underline{\quad}$$
$$2, 23, \underline{\quad}$$
$$3, 22, \underline{\quad}$$
$$4, 21, \underline{\quad}$$
$$5, 20, \underline{\quad}$$
$$6, 19, \underline{\quad}$$

84. CHECKER PIECES

Below is an odd-shaped piece of a checkerboard. Can you divide it along the lines into two identical parts?

(The two pieces are identical in shape, but not necessarily identical in terms of dark and light squares.)

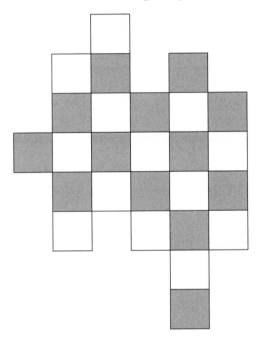

85. HOOK AND LADDER

A 25-foot ladder is leaning against a building so that the top of the ladder is 24 feet off the ground. Suppose the ladder slides down so that its top is only 20 feet off the ground. How far must the bottom of the ladder have slid out along the ground?

86. CUBIC'S RUBE

Only one of the following three shapes cannot be bent on its edges to form a cube. Which one, the top, middle, or bottom one?

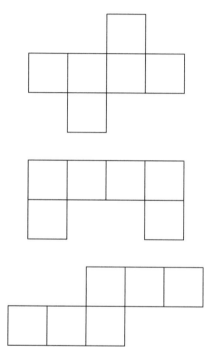

87. AGENT 99

Place addition signs between some of the digits below in such a way that the sum equals 99. There are two solutions.

$$9 \quad 8 \quad 7 \quad 6 \quad 5 \quad 4 \quad 3 \quad 2 \quad 1 = 99$$

88. ONE, TWO, THREE, FOUR

Four boxes are arranged as in the diagram below. Place some number of × marks in each box so that the total number of ×'s in pairs of boxes that are connected to one another equals 1, 2, 3, and 4 (not necessarily in order) as you go around the diagram.

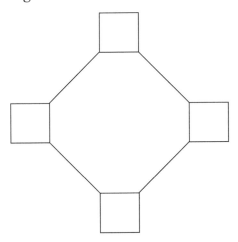

89. TRICKY COMBINATIONS

Using the digits 1, 3, 4, and 6, can you form each of the numbers 20 through 30 using only the standard operations of addition, subtraction, multiplication, and division?

We'll even start you off:

$$20 = (6 + 4) \times (3 - 1)$$
$$21 = 31 - 6 - 4$$

You're on your own for the rest of them!

90. CUTTING CORNERS

A 5 × 5 square has its corners cut off as in the diagram below:

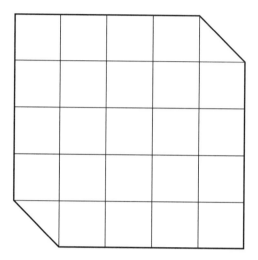

By making precisely one continuous cut, divide the figure into two pieces that can be reassembled to produce a 4 × 6 rectangle. (The interior lines are just for reference. They do not need to be preserved in the dissection process.)

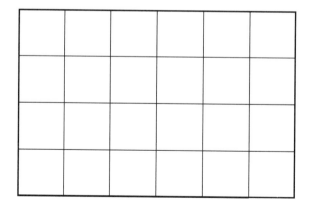

91. AS THE CROW FLIES

Thelma and Louise were standing on a street corner trying to decide which of two New York City restaurants to go to, Alfredo's or Bernardo's. They eventually decided to eat at Alfredo's, because it was two blocks closer. However, two crows were listening in on the entire conversation, and to them the decision made no sense; from the crows' point of view, Alfredo's and Bernardo's were exactly the same distance away.

Assuming the city blocks to be perfectly square, and assuming that neither restaurant was on the street or avenue that Thelma and Louise were already on, how far away were each of the two restaurants?

92. COUNTIN' IN THE RAIN

On a certain island, the rainfall follows a very reliable pattern: If it rains in the morning, it is clear in the afternoon. One family comes to the island for their vacation. When they leave, they realize that it has rained 15 times altogether. There were 12 clear mornings and 13 clear afternoons. How long was their vacation?

93. REVERSAL OF FORTUNE

Can you come up with a pair of numbers X and Y, each less than 100, such that $X + Y$ is the "reversal" of $X \times Y$?

For example, if both X and Y equal 9, we get $9 + 9 = 18$ and $9 \times 9 = 81$. Note that 18 and 81 are reversals of one another. Your job is to come up with a pair of numbers X and Y that are not equal to one another. There are two different pairs of numbers that work. Can you find them?

94. ORDER IN THE COURTS

The Minnesota State Tennis Championships was looking for a new site. Tournament organizers uncovered a surveyor's map for a piece of farmland that they were considering purchasing. They wanted to put as many courts as they could within the plot of land—all the while adhering to the strictest regulations of the United States Tennis Association. The recommended dimensions for a tennis court, including the areas behind the baselines and alongside the sidelines, turned out to be 120 feet long by 60 feet wide. How many courts could they fit within the plot of land? (Be careful!)

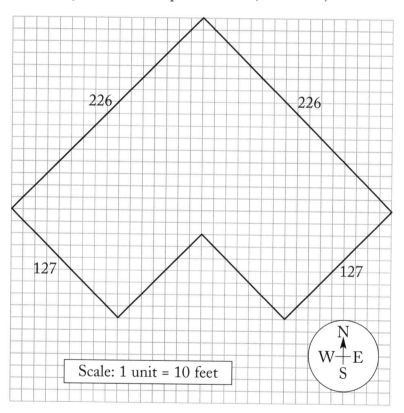

226   226

127   127

Scale: 1 unit = 10 feet

95. COLORING BOXES

The box below forms the basis for a game between two players. The idea is that the two players take turns shading in one of the six rectangles with one of two colors—say, red or blue. Either player can use either color on any turn. It is illegal to shade a rectangle with a color that has already been given to a neighboring rectangle. If you don't have a legal move at your turn, you lose the game.

Show that for each opening move by the first player, the second player can always win.

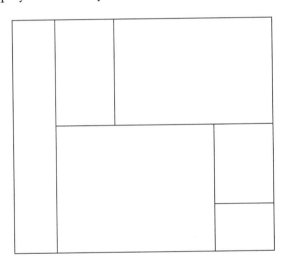

96. EASIER BY THE DOZEN

Can you come up with the nine pairs of whole numbers (X,Y) that satisfy this equation?

$$\frac{XY}{X+Y} = 10$$

97. A REGAL CHALLENGE

Your challenge is to rearrange the letters R E G A L to form another common English word. Sound too easy? Well, there are a couple of hitches. First of all, you must make the transformation in individual "moves," where a move consists of interchanging two consecutive letters, as from R E G A L to R G E A L. The second hitch is that you must complete the transformation in an *odd* number of moves. Can you do it?

98. CIVIL DISOBEDIENCE

The word CIVIL consists entirely of Roman numerals. Although the word taken as a whole doesn't satisfy the rules of Roman numerals, it is possible to select one or more letters from CIVIL, without changing their order, so as to produce legitimate Roman numeral constructions: for example, CVI = 106. (In case you're wondering, a standard Roman numeral is built by splitting its Arabic version into place values and translating piece by piece. For example, 49 splits into 40 + 9, so its Roman numeral equivalent is XLIX, not IL.)

In all, 13 such numbers can be created from CIVIL. Is the sum of those 13 numbers odd or even? (You don't need to list them in order to get the answer.)

99. WHEN WE MEET AGAIN

At the stroke of noon, the hands of a clock are of course pointed in the exact same direction. How much time goes by before this happens again?

100. THREE'S COMPANY

It's easy to express the number 9 using precisely three 3's if you're allowed plus signs: $9 = 3 + 3 + 3$. But can you do it without using plus signs? That's the challenge: Using any mathematical symbols you like *except* plus signs, find *three* different ways to express the number 9 using precisely three 3's and no other digits.

Answers

1. LAZY DAYS OF SUMMER

The 24 four-digit numbers that can be formed using the digits 1, 2, 3, and 4 sum to 66,660.

To obtain this sum without adding up the 24 numbers, note that each column of the sum involves six 1's, six 2's, six 3's, and six 4's. The sum of these 24 digits in each column is $6 \times (1 + 2 + 3 + 4) = 6 \times 10 = 60$. Therefore, to obtain the sum in question, you line up the 60's in each of the four columns and add:

$$
\begin{array}{r}
60 \\
60 \\
60 \\
\underline{60} \\
66660
\end{array}
$$

2. PIECES OF EIGHT

The length of a side of a smaller cube is four units, or one-half the side of the big cube.

3. SOMETHING IS MISSING

3	11	21	41	91
6	14	15	23	53
3	5	6	8	12

The third row is obtained by adding together the numbers

in the first two rows and then taking the square root. (3 is the square root of 3 + 6 = 9; similarly 5 is the square root of 11 + 14 = 25, etc.) The missing number is therefore 12, because 91 + 53 = 144, and 12 is the square root of 144.

4. SEEING SPOTS

Three spots are in the center—one each for the 1, 3, and 5 faces. Sixteen spots are in the corners—for the 2 (two), 3 (two), 4 (four), 5 (four), and 6 (four) faces. That leaves two spots for the sides, and both of these are found on the 6 face.

5. FILL IN THE BLANKS

$$12 \div 2 + 7 - 4 = 9$$

6. HOW FAR?

To prove that a given number is prime, you only need to check as far as the largest prime number less than its square root. Why? Because in any pair of factors for the number, one factor will be greater than the square root and the other factor will be less. (If the number is a perfect square, then it will have two factors that equal one another, but we're not going to waste our time showing that a perfect square isn't prime!) The point is that if you haven't come across a factor by the time you reach the square root, you never will. In the case of 907, the largest whole number less than the square root of 907 is 30, and so the largest prime you need to consider is 29.

7. MARY, QUITE CONTRARY

The third statement is the most likely. The principle at work is that any one event is more likely than that same event plus another one. The three statements turn out to be ordered from least likely to most likely.

The reason the answer is surprising is that if you came across someone named Mary who satisfied all of the conditions in the first statement, you'd feel she had a much better chance of being the Mary you grew up with than if all you knew was that she went bowling on Tuesday nights. But that's not what was asked!

8. ON ALL FOURS

148 is the answer. To arrive at this answer, simply start dividing a string of 4's by 3 until you get no remainder.

When you start dividing, you see that 3 goes into 4 once, with a remainder of 1. Bring down a 4, making 14. Then 3 goes into 14 four times, with a remainder of 2. Bring down another 4, making 24. 3 goes into 24 precisely 8 times, so 444 divided by 3 equals 148.

9. GAME OF THE CENTURY

Player A can always win the game by calling out "1" at the first turn. After that, whatever Player B adds, Player A then adds 11 minus that number. In this fashion, Player A will call out "12," "23," "34," and so on. This sequence consists of all numbers that are one greater than a multiple of 11. Because 100 is a member of this sequence ($100 = 9 \times 11 + 1$), Player A is guaranteed to win the game.

10. DON'T LEAVE ME OUT

If Jerry was not on the starting team, he would be one of two players who were left out. There are six others overall, and each of these six could be paired with Jerry to sit out, so there are six teams that do *not* include Jerry as a starter.

Because there are 21 possible teams in all, Jerry must be a starter on 21 − 6 = 15 of those teams.

Where does the 21 come from? It comes up because 21 = $^7\!/(5!)(2!)$, where $n!$ equals the product of all whole numbers from 1 to n inclusive. The idea is that when choosing a team, you have 7 choices for the first player, 6 choices for the second player, and so on, down to 3 choices for the fifth player. But because the order in which you selected the team doesn't matter, you have to divide by the total number of ways of arranging the five players, which is 5!. (In other words, the team you got by choosing Alex, Brian, Clifford, Dave, and Elmer is the same as the team you would have gotten by choosing Dave, Brian, Elmer, Alex, and Clifford.)

11. SO FAR, YET SO CLOSE

The plus sign has been changed to a 4!

$$5+545=550$$

12. DOUBLY TRUE

The solutions are as follows:

$$
\begin{array}{r}
5\,0 \\
+\ 5\,0 \\
\hline
1\,0\,0
\end{array}
$$

The largest carryover possible when adding two numbers is 1, so C must equal 1. In the right column, the only possibility is $I = 0$. Since $L + L = 10$, we see that $L = 5$.

$$
\begin{array}{r}
5\ 8\ 1 \\
5\ 8\ 1 \\
+\ 9\ 2\ 3\ 1 \\
\hline
1\ 0\ 3\ 9\ 3
\end{array}
$$

The only carryover possible in the leftmost column is 1, so $S = 1$. Since $S = 1$, then from the rightmost column, $E = 3$. In the column second from the right, there is no carryover brought into it, so $O + O + 3$ sums to a number ending in T. This means T is an odd number, so (from column 2) T must be 9. Since $T = 9$, then O must be 8 and I must be 0. From this point, trying the various possibilities shows that only $D = 5$ and $R = 2$ finish the puzzle.

13. WAGERING ABOVEBOARD

If the second man has a net gain of three dollars but lost three games in the process, then overall he must have won six games and lost three. Since there were no draws, this is a total of nine games played.

14. RUN-ON SENTENCE

The number of 0's in this box is 1.

The number of 1's in this box is 7.

The number of 2's in this box is 3.

The number of 3's in this box is 2.

The number of 4's in this box is 1.

The number of 5's in this box is 1.

The number of 6's in this box is 1.

The number of 7's in this box is 2.

The number of 8's in this box is 1.

The number of 9's in this box is 1.

15. DIVIDING LINE

The line is two miles from Braddock. Note that the triangle has an area of four square miles—one-half the "base" of eight miles times the "height" of one mile. At the point two miles from Braddock, the smaller right triangle to the right of the diagram has one side equal to six miles and the other side equal to $\frac{2}{3}$ of a mile (because you are one-third the way from Alton to Clancy at the point where the north-south line intersects your path). The product of 6 and $\frac{2}{3}$ is 4, and dividing by two gives an area for the triangle on the right of two square miles, as it should be.

16. TEACHERS' SPAT

The math teacher noticed that 1, 4, and 7 were the only digits to leave a remainder of 1 upon dividing by 3. The art teacher noticed that 1, 4, and 7 were the only digits that could be formed by using straight lines only. Each of the numbers in the second group requires a curved line.

17. HEAD START

Let P equal the probability that Chris will win the game. To compute P, we start by noting that obviously the game is over if Chris flips "heads" on the first try, and that will happen with probability ½.

If Chris flips "tails" (probability ½) there is also a probability of ½ that Jean will flip "tails," in which case the game would return to how it was at the beginning. The combined probability of Chris and Jean flipping "tails" equals ¼. The equation that expresses all of the above is that $P = ½ + ¼(P)$.

Solving the equation yields $(¾)P = ½$, so $P = ⅔$.

For another method, note that the probability is ½ that Chris will win immediately. But if that doesn't happen, Jean is in the same position that Chris was in originally, so her chance of winning is precisely ½ of his chance. Since the two probabilities must add to 1, the only possible solution is that Chris's probability of winning is ⅔ and Jean's chance is ⅓.

18. PLAYING THE TRIANGLE

The third side must have length 17. The only other choice is that the length of the third side is 8 (remember, the triangle is isosceles, so two sides have the same length). However, a length of 8 is impossible, because if two sides of a triangle were both 8, they could never reach the third side (length 17), even if laid end to end! (In general, the sum of any two sides of a triangle must be greater than the third side. This principle is called the "triangle inequality.")

19. TAKING THE NINTH

The last digit of the ninth power of any number is the same as the last digit of the number itself! This fact is shown in the chart below. Once you observe that the nine huge numbers in the problem all end with different digits, it's easy to arrive at the answer. Just put them in order by their last digits.

0	1	2	3	4	5	6	7	8	9	original number's last digit
0	1	4	9	6	5	6	9	4	1	
0	1	8	7	4	5	6	3	2	9	
0	1	6	1	6	5	6	1	6	1	
0	1	2	3	4	5	6	7	8	9	last digit of fifth power
0	1	4	9	6	5	6	9	4	1	
0	1	8	7	4	5	6	3	2	9	
0	1	6	1	6	5	6	1	6	1	
0	1	2	3	4	5	6	7	8	9	last digit of ninth power

The ninth row shows that ninth powers end in the same digit as the original numbers. The fifth row shows that fifth powers have the same property. In fact, the chart repeats in blocks of four, which shows that the $(4n + 1)$th power of any number ends in the same digit as the original number.

20. AVERAGES MADE EASY

$^{(4 + 5)}\!/_2 = 4.5$

Similarly, $^{(49 + 50)}\!/_2 = 49.50$, $^{(499 + 500)}\!/_2 = 499.500$, and so on.

21. SIZES AND SHAPES

The diameter of the smaller circle equals one-half the diameter of the larger circle.

An easy way to see this result is to draw another triangle inside the smaller circle. Clearly this triangle is one-fourth the size of the larger triangle, so, since the proportions of the triangles and circles don't change, the smaller circle must be precisely one-fourth the size of the larger one. But that means the radius (and therefore the diameter) of the larger circle must be twice as big as the radius of the small circle, because the formula Area = πr^2 means that doubling the radius of a circle will multiply its area by four.

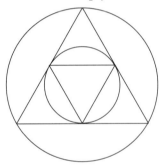

22. MY THREE SONS

The equation is $x + (x + 3) + (x + 6) = 57$, where x is the age of the youngest son. This simplifies to $3x = 48$, so $x = 16$. The sons are therefore 16, 19, and 22 years old.

Alternatively, the man's age must be three times the age of the middle son, because the other sons are spaced equally to either side. The middle son is therefore $57/3 = 19$ years of age.

23. WATER UNDER THE BRIDGE

If you keep getting 19 minutes, you are forgiven. There are two things you need to realize in order to get the 17-minute solution. The first is that it's most efficient for the two slowest men to cross together. And the second, harder-to-see realization is that you can get the two slowest men across without having to send them each separately with the fastest man to bring the flashlight back. The secret lies in having someone faster already waiting on the other side to bring the flashlight back when the slower men arrive together.

Here's a 17-minute plan (#1 stands for the one-minute crosser, etc.):

	Steps	Time	Total elapsed time
1)	#1 and #2 cross	2 min.	2 min.
2)	#1 crosses back	1 min.	3 min.
3)	#5 and #10 cross	10 min.	13 min.
4)	#2 crosses back	2 min.	15 min.
5)	#1 and #2 cross	2 min.	17 min.

You could also have #2 cross back in the second step and #1 cross back in the fourth step. The total elapsed time remains the same.

24. LUCKY 13

One possible solution is as follows:

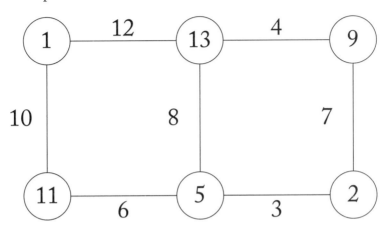

25. PRIME MOVERS

The smallest number that cannot be made prime by changing a single digit is 200. Note that the only possible change that might produce a prime number would be to alter the last digit, but $201 = 3 \times 67$, $203 = 7 \times 29$, $207 = 9 \times 23$, and $209 = 29 \times 11$, while the other numbers between 200 and 210 end in either 5 or an even number and are therefore composite.

26. A BURNING PROBLEM

Burn one of the wicks to get the first hour. Now you have two wicks remaining and 45 minutes to measure. The first "Aha!" is realizing that, despite the varying burning rate, if you light any wick at both ends, the wick's burning time is cut precisely in half. So if you light one of the two remaining wicks at both ends, it will burn for exactly half an hour. (Get it? If it burns for longer or shorter than half an hour, then the two halves did not add up to an hour's worth of burning time, as originally stated.)

So now you can time one and a half hours using two wicks. But how do you get the final fifteen minutes? Well, you need to think laterally. Here's how to do it: When you light both ends of the second wick, also light one end of the third wick. When the second wick has burned completely, the third wick will have half an hour's time left to burn. Then, light its other end, and you'll cut its remaining time in half, giving you 15 minutes exactly.

27. SUM-DAY SOON

A) The last sum-day of the 21st century is December 31, 2043, because 12 + 31 = 43, and both the month and the day are as big as possible.

B) This one is much easier than you might think. The correct answer is 365, because every day in a standard (non-leap) year is part of a sum-day for *some* year. (For example, November 26 is a sum-day for the year 2037, because 11 + 26 = 37.) The only date for which this principle doesn't work is the leap day, February 29. That's because 2 + 29 = 31, but 2031 is not a leap year.

28. CUBIC MEASURE

Along each edge of the cube there are exactly three cubes colored on two sides. Since a cube has 12 edges, there are precisely 12 × 3 = 36 cubes with exactly two green faces.

29. HOW NOW, BROWN COW?

If BL is the daily production of the black cow and BR is the daily production of the brown cow, then 5(4BL + 3BR) = 4(3BL + 5BR). Multiplying this out gives 20BL + 15BR = 12BL + 20BR. Simplifying gives 8BL = 5BR, so 5 brown cows produce as much each day as eight black cows. The brown cows are therefore more productive.

30. UNLIKELY RESULT

The most likely event is A)—getting heads at least once from the flipping of two coins. The probability of this happening is ¾, because the only way you don't get heads at least once is to get both tails, and that event has probability (½)(½) = ¼.

By comparison, if you flip four coins, there are 16 possible outcomes altogether, and there are five ways of getting heads once or fewer. (There are four different coins that could come up heads, plus one chance in sixteen that all could come up tails.) That makes a probability of ¹¹⁄₁₆ that you get at least two heads, and ¹¹⁄₁₆ is just a hair less than ¾. Similar logic reveals that the other two outcomes (three heads from six coins and four heads from eight coins) are even less likely.

31. CLOSE, BUT NO CIGAR

Jurgen's actual score was 96. Note that 20 percent of 80 equals 16. Jurgen's score was 16 points higher than Ian's, so in that sense he did 20 percent better.

The confusion was caused by the fact that most people don't really use percentages in that fashion. When we say "percent," we often mean "percentage point." Once you say that Jurgen did "16 percentage points better" instead of "20 percent better," there is no confusion.

32. THE KNIGHT'S TOUR

9	6	1	4
♞	3	10	7
11	8	5	2

Above is one way in which the knight can get around the entire 3 × 4 board. The final stop is the bottom left square. This is the only possible square that the knight can end up on.

The starting square is white, and the squares numbered 8 and 2 in the above diagram are also white. But the knight could never end up on either of these squares, because each move of the knight brings it from either white to black or black to white, so 11 moves must leave it on the opposite color from where it started.

Square 5 is also impossible as a resting place, for a somewhat different reason. If the knight could end up on square 5, it could return to its starting place with one more move. But such a "closed" tour has been shown to be impossible on a 3 × 4 board. Without this piece of knowledge, you wouldn't know which square, 5 or 11, was the correct answer. But since the problem states that there is only one possible solution, all you needed to do was find any possible sequence that ends in the bottom row. Since ending on square 5 is impossible, any sequence you found must have ended on square 11.

33. THE PICKY EATERS CLUB

There are 28 club members who have tried cauliflower and 19 who have tried spinach, for an apparent total of 47. But the 15 who have tried both cauliflower and spinach are counted twice in this total; eliminating that duplication gives a total of 32 members who have tried either cauliflower or spinach. That leaves 100 − 32 = 68 members who haven't tried either one. All told, the club members break down as follows:

      68 have never tried cauliflower or spinach

       4 have tried spinach only

      13 have tried cauliflower only

      <u>15</u> have tried both spinach and cauliflower

100 total

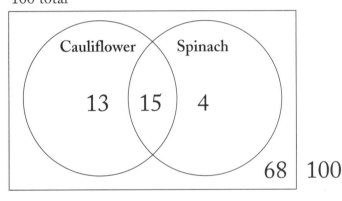

34. THE USUAL SUSPECTS

We can only have one true statement. Try each statement in order.

If Alan's statement is true, then so is Charlie's.

If Bill's statement is true, then so is Charlie's.

If Charlie's statement is true, then so is Don's.

None of these three can be telling the truth by himself, as the question requires. So Don must be telling the truth and therefore Charlie did the robbery.

35. BORDERLINE CASE

Two colors are all you would need to fill in *any* map consisting of intersecting lines. Simply start by shading in the upper left corner, then shade in the region that meets the upper left region in a single point. Follow that same pattern the whole way through, and you will have shaded in every region with an "×" in it.

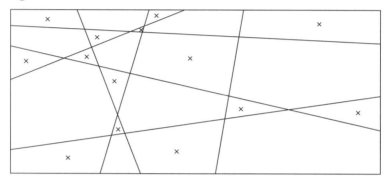

36. FILL IN THE BOXES

10	11	20	21	22	23	42
9	12	19	18	17	24	41
8	13	14	15	16	25	40
7	30	29	28	27	26	39
6	31	32	33	34	35	38
5	4	3	2	1	36	37

This puzzle was conceived by Sidney Kravitz.

37. PARENTHETICAL MENTION

$$2 + (2 \times 2) - (2/2) = 5$$
$$(2 + 2) \times 2 - (2/2) = 7$$
$$(2 + 2) \times (2 - (2/2)) = 4$$

Technically, you don't need any parentheses for A), because multiplication and division must be performed *before* addition and subtraction. That's the rule!

38. NICKEL ARCADE

The probability of winning the game is less than 10 percent, so C) is the correct answer.

It is tempting to conclude that the probability of winning is simply the ratio of the area of all the circles divided by the area of the rectangle. That would make for a probability of $15\pi/(22 \times 14) = 15\pi/308$, or about 153 chances in 1000—15.3 percent. But the actual probability is quite a bit lower than that. Here's why:

In order to win the game, the center of the nickel must come to rest within an imaginary smaller circle nested inside one of the larger ones. The diameter of one of those smaller circles is one inch, so its area is $\pi/4$ square inches. There are 15 circles altogether, so the total "winning area" is $15\pi/4$ square inches. On the other hand, the total area of the rectangle in which the center of the circle might fall is 21×13, or 273 square inches. (The entire board is 22×14, but the center cannot possibly land within $\frac{1}{2}"$ of the border, as indicated by the dotted line.) The probability of success is therefore $15\pi/(4 \times 273)$, or 43 chances in 1000—only 4.3 percent!

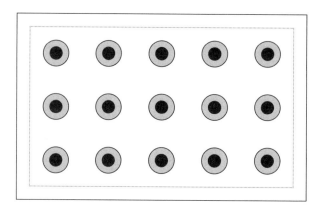

39. EIGHT IS ENOUGH

The partition below works for the first eight integers.

| 1, 2, 4, 8 | | 3, 5, 6, 7 |

The solution happens to be unique. For example, suppose that 2 were in the right-hand box instead. Then we would soon reach an impossible position: If 3 were in the left, then 4 would have to be in the right (because otherwise there would be no place for 6, because 1 and 5 would be in the left and 2 and 4 would be in the right). But then 6 would have to be in the left (2 and 4 are already in the right), making the placement of 7 impossible. Phew! By repeating this type of logic, the above partition can be proved unique. In particular, it is impossible to make a partition that works for the first *nine* integers, because there is nowhere for 9 to go!

40. FIND THE SHORTCUT

Since 5 cubed is 125, 50 cubed must be 125,000. Similarly, 60 cubed is 216,000. Note that 148,877 is in between 125,000 and 216,000, so if 148,877 is the cube of some whole number, that number must be between 50 and 60. But the only way the cube of a number can end in 7 is if the original number ends in 3. See the portion of the table from answer #19 below:

0	1	2	3	4	5	6	7	8	9	original number's last digit
0	1	4	9	6	5	6	9	4	1	last digit of square
0	1	8	7	4	5	6	3	2	9	last digit of cube

Therefore the cube root of 148,877 must be 53.

41. MISSED ONE!

The only decade of the 20th century that lacks a multiple of 11 is the 1970s. The key step is to notice that the only way a decade could lack a multiple of 11 is for the first year of the following decade to be a multiple of 11, which reduces to examining the numbers from 191 through 200 (the final zero doesn't contribute to a number's divisibility by 11). The only multiple of 11 among this group is 198—note that the outer two digits add up to the middle digit, which is characteristic of certain multiples of 11. Therefore the decade prior to 1980 is the one we want.

42. THE MERRY-GO-ROUND

Any solution to the puzzle must be a variation of the one below. In all solutions, the center circle must be 1. The other eight numbers are split into four pairs, each of which adds up to 11. The sum of the three numbers along any line is 12.

The sum of the numbers from 1 to 9 is 45. We need to remove one number from this total (for the central number in the diagram) and be left with four equal sums. So we need to subtract a digit from 45 and be left with a multiple of 4. The only three digits that we can subtract from 45 to leave a multiple of 4 are 1, 5, and 9. If 5 or 9 were the middle number, then it wouldn't be possible to make the row total be a multiple of 4. So the center number must be 1 and the remaining numbers sum to 44, so each pair surrounding the 1 must total 11.

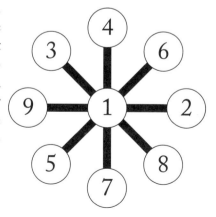

68

43. JUST FOR FUN

A) $2^5 \times 9^2 = 2592$

B) $6 + 6 + 6 + (6 \times 6 \times 6) + (6 \times 6 \times 6) + (6 \times 6 \times 6) = 666$

C) $12^2 + 33^2 = 1233$

D) $(3 + 4 + 0 + 1 + 2 + 2 + 2 + 4)^6 = 34{,}012{,}224$

E) $4! + 0! + 5! + 8! + 5! = 40{,}585$

F) $3^3 + 4^4 + 3^3 + 5^5 = 3435$

44. TARGET PRACTICE

Assume that the radius of the bull's-eye is 1. The area of the bull's-eye is therefore π. The area of the outside black ring is $\pi 5^2 - \pi 4^2 = 9\pi$, so the sum is 10π. Similarly, the area of the smaller white ring is 3π and the area of the larger white ring is 7π, so both add up to 10π.

45. CANDY LAND

The number of candies in the first box is not divisible by three, so the number of candies in the first box must be of the form $3k + 1$ or $3k + 2$ for some whole number k. Let's consider these two cases one by one.

If there are $3k + 2$ candies in the first box, then the second box contains $3k + 12$ candies. But this can't be right, because we were told that the students couldn't share the candies in the second box equally, and $3k + 12$ is divisible by 3.

If instead there are $3k + 1$ candies in the first box, the number of candies in the second box is $3k + 11$ (which is okay, because it isn't divisible by 3) and the number of candies in both boxes is $(3k + 1) + (3k + 11) = 6k + 12$. Since we can write $6k + 12$ as $3(2k + 4)$, we know that this is divisible by 3, as required.

46. ALL IN THE NEIGHBORHOOD

Sarah will be four times as old in just five days.

Sarah is always 24 days older than Melanie. To be four times as old as Melanie, this difference of 24 days must be three times Melanie's age. Since $^{24}/_3 = 8$, when Melanie is 8 days old, Sarah will be four times older at 32 days. Since Melanie will be 8 days old in five days, the answer is five days from today.

47. MATCHSTICK MATCH

By adding the 10 matchsticks as in the diagram below, the yard is divided into five L-shaped plots, in addition to the square house we started with.

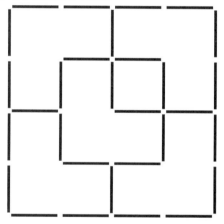

48. THROUGH THE LOOKING GLASS

There are many, many palindrome years you could use for this problem. Here are a few examples:
A) 110 years apart — 1771 and 1881
B) 11 years apart — 1991 and 2002
C) 10 years apart — 575 and 585
D) 2 years apart — 99 and 101

49. FULL OF HOT AIR

The red balloon was the highest. Using algebra, our equations are as follows:

$$R + B = 140$$
$$B + Y = 135$$
$$R + Y = 155$$

A neat way to solve symmetric equations like this is to add all three together. Here, we get:

$$2R + 2Y + 2B = 430, \text{ so}$$
$$R + Y + B = 215.$$

Now that we have the sum of the three heights, we can simply subtract each of the three original equations from it in turn to find the individual values. We get $R = 80$, $Y = 75$, and $B = 60$.

50. NIFTY FIFTY

From the information in the question, we can write the equations:

$$3G + 5Y = 41$$
$$G + Y = 9$$

Subtracting 3 times the second equation from the first gives $2Y = 14$, so $Y = 7$. Ben has 2 green cards and 7 yellow cards, for a total of $(3 \times 2) + (5 \times 7) = 41$ points.

51. TEN-LETTER DAY

There are many solutions to this problem. Here is one:

$$
\begin{array}{r}
1\ 5\ 7 \\
3\ 6\ 0 \\
+\ 4\ 8\ 2 \\
\hline
9\ 9\ 9
\end{array}
$$

52. ODDS-ON FAVORITE

Remember, A, B, and C are the only runners in the race. If P equals the probability that C will win, then the probability that B will win equals $2P$, and the probability that A will win equals $4P$.

Altogether, we have $4P + 2P + P = 1$, because it is certain (probability 1) that one of the three will win. Therefore, $P = \frac{1}{7}$, and the probability that A will win is $4P = \frac{4}{7}$.

53. MAKING EVERYONE HAPPY

The situation described by Mr. Townsend is not only possible, it is remarkably simple. Suppose that the class had been given three tests during the term. On the first, the scores of the three students in question—abbreviated A, B, and C—followed the pattern A > B > C. On the second test, the pattern was B > C > A, while on the third test, the pattern was C > A > B.

You can see that A beat B two-thirds of the time, B beat C two-thirds of the time, and C beat A two-thirds of the time!

54. ONE THROUGH NINE

Here is one solution:

$$8 - 1 = 7$$
$$6 \div 3 = 2$$
$$4 + 5 = 9$$

55. SQUARE DEAL

Here are squares divided into six smaller squares and seven smaller squares:

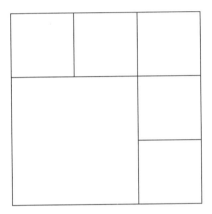

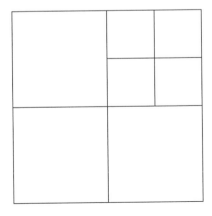

56. LION IN WAITING

The sheep lives! To see why, first suppose that there were only one lion and one sheep. In that case, the sheep would get eaten, because even though the lion knew he would become drowsy and vulnerable upon eating the sheep, there would be no other lion there to take advantage.

However, if there were two lions, everything would change. In that case, neither lion would dare eat the sheep, because he would become a meal for the other lion.

If there were three lions, then again the sheep would be eaten—by whichever lion could get there first. Why does this happen? Because neither of the two other lions would dare eat the lion that ate the sheep (this solution is starting to sound like a nursery rhyme), for the same reason that spared the sheep in the case where we had two lions!

If you keep going in this same way, you'll see that the sheep will always be eaten if the number of lions is odd, and the sheep will always survive if the number of lions is even. Because 16 is an even number, the sheep lives.

57. NO SQUARING REQUIRED

The area of the triangle is $^{(3 \times 4)}/_2$ = 6 square units. The area of the rectangle is twice the area of the triangle. The area of the rectangle is its length times its height, so its height must be $^{12}/_5$.

58. JUST FOR KICKS

The highest score that cannot be achieved using only converted touchdowns (7 points) and field goals (3 points) is 11.

We can certainly make the scores 12 (by using 4 field goals), 13 (one touchdown and 2 field goals), and 14 (two touchdowns). Now consider this chart of possible scores arranged in rows of three:

```
 1   2   3
 4   5   6
 7   8   9
10  11  12
13  14  15
16  17  18  ...
```

Since we can make scores of 12, 13, and 14, we can make any score below them in their respective columns by adding the appropriate number of field goals. This proves that every score after 11 can be made with touchdowns and field goals. A little trial and error will prove that 11 cannot be made, so 11 is the highest number that cannot be made by adding 7's and 3's.

In general, if A and B are whole numbers that do not have a common factor, the highest number that cannot be produced by a combination of A's and B's equals $AB - A - B$. In this case $A = 7$ and $B = 3$, so $AB - A - B = 21 - 7 - 3 = 11$.

59. THE A&P

If L and W are the length and width of the rectangle, then we can solve as follows, using a neat factoring trick:

$$LW = 2L + 2W$$
$$LW - 2L - 2W = 0$$
$$LW - 2L - 2W + 4 = 4$$
$$(L - 2)(W - 2) = 4$$

Since L and W are whole numbers, we can match $(L - 2)$ and $(W - 2)$ with factors of 4. Since 4 factors as both 4×1 and 2×2, we get two solutions:

$L - 2 = 4$ and $W - 2 = 1$ (so $L = 6$ and $W = 3$) or
$L - 2 = 2$ and $W - 2 = 2$ (so $L = 4$ and $W = 4$)

There are two solutions: a 4×4 square or a 6×3 rectangle.

60. RADICAL MOVEMENT

$5\frac{5}{24} = \frac{125}{24} = 25(\frac{5}{24})$. The square root of this equals 5 times the square root of $\frac{5}{24}$, so the two expressions are equal!

61. DIVIDING LINES

$111{,}111 = 11 \times 10{,}101$. A similar factoring can be made of any number that consists of an *even* number of 1's. However, a number consisting of an *odd* number of 1's— such as 11,111—is not divisible by 11.

62. PROOF IN THE PUDDING

April came first and ate one-third of the pudding. Mike came second and ate one-half of what he saw, which happened to be one-third of what was there originally. Sarah came last and ate everything she saw, which also happened to be one-third of what was there originally.

63. BOXING MATCH

The first box will fit more. The height of the first box equals $6 \; [= (18 - 6) \div 2]$, so its volume equals $6 \times 6 \times 6 = 216$ square units. The height of the second box equals $3 \; [= (14 - 8) \div 2]$, so its volume equals $8 \times 8 \times 3 = 192$ square units.

64. ODD QUESTION

The last three-digit number is 999, and the last two-digit number is 99, so there are $999 - 99 = 900$ three-digit numbers, of which half are odd. That means there are 450 odd three-digit numbers.

For another method, note that there are nine possibilities for the hundreds digit (no 0 is possible), ten possibilities for the tens digit (no restrictions), and 5 possibilities for the ones digit (the last digit must be odd). That gives a total of $9 \times 10 \times 5 = 450$ numbers.

65. SIX-SHOOTER

The only way that a number can be divisible by 6 is if it is divisible by both 2 and 3. Note that $n(n + 1)(2n + 1)$ is always divisible by 2, because either n or $n + 1$ must be even. As for divisibility by 3, the problem becomes similar to #45. If n is divisible by 3, we're all done. If n leaves a remainder of 2 upon division by 3, then $n + 1$ must be divisible by 3. And if n leaves a remainder of 1 upon division by 3 (the only other possibility), then $2n + 1$ must be divisible by 3. Any way you slice it, $n(n + 1)(2n + 1)$ is divisible by 2 and 3, and therefore by 6.

By the way, $n(n + 1)(2n + 1)/6$ equals the sum of the *squares* of the first n whole numbers, so it's always a whole number!

66. LOOK BEFORE YOU LEAP

The area of the rectangle is increased by 300 percent. Note that an increase of 100 percent for a side of the rectangle is the same as doubling it. Doubling both sides multiplies the area by four. And multiplying a number by four is the same as increasing it by 300 percent—not 400 percent!

67. BARNYARD COLLAGE

There is only one combination that works: 5 cows, 1 pig, and 94 sheep.

The conditions of the problem produce the following two equations:

$$20C + 6P + S = 200$$
$$C + P + S = 100$$

Multiplying the second equation by six and subtracting, we get $14C - 5S = -400$. Rearranging, $14C = 5S - 400$. This means that $14C$ is divisible by 5, and therefore so is C. But $C = 10$ is impossible, because buying 10 cows would use up all of the money. And $C = 0$ is impossible because at least one of each animal must be purchased. The only conceivable choice is therefore $C = 5$. The rest of the solution follows immediately.

68. STRANGE SEQUENCE

The last number in the sequence is 5. The rule for the sequence is that each number is the position in the alphabet of the letters in the word SEQUENCE. S is the 19th letter, E is the 5th letter, Q is the 17th letter, and so on.

69. SMALL BUT POWERFUL

If a number is both a perfect square and a perfect cube, then it is a perfect sixth power. The next sixth power after $1^6 = 1$ is $2^6 = 64$, which is both 8^2 and 4^3. The next sixth power is $3^6 = 729$, which is both 27^2 and 9^3.

70. A BRIDGE TOO FAR

The East-West pair holds a total of 26 cards, 4 of which are diamonds. (North and South together hold the other 9 diamonds.) That leaves 22 cards for the other three suits. Even if 21 of them are split equally 7–7–7 among the other three suits, the 22nd card will be the eighth card in its suit, so one suit must consist of at least 8 cards.

71. BYE BYE BIRDIE

Seven byes will do the trick. The idea is to have the second round consist of 32 players, because 32 is a power of two. (32 = 2 to the fifth power, and it is the biggest power of two less than 57.) In order to achieve this outcome, we must play 57 − 32 = 25 matches, because one player is eliminated with every match. If there are 25 matches, this accounts for 50 players, so we must give the other 7 players a bye into the second round.

Once you see how this works, the simpler method is to subtract 57 from the next highest power of 2, which happens to be 64. We get 64 − 57 = 7, as before.

72. BE PERFECTLY FRANK

Five hot dogs (intermission) plus four hot dogs (left over) equals just one-eighth of his original supply, because we know that a total of seven-eighths was sold during the game itself. That means the vendor must have started the soccer game with 9 × 8 = 72 hot dogs.

73. THE CHRISTMAS CYCLE

To count the total number of presents, we need to add up 12 × 1 (the partridges), 11 × 2 (the turtle doves), 10 × 3 (the French hens), and so forth, all the way to 1 × 12 for the drummers drumming. One way to perform this addition is to do it one row at a time, as follows:

$$1 = 1$$
$$1 + 2 = 3$$
$$1 + 2 + 3 = 6$$
$$1 + 2 + 3 + 4 = 10$$

Note that 1 + 3 = 4, which happens to be two squared. Similarly, 6 + 10 = 16, which happens to be four squared.

79

Continuing in this fashion, the sum for the 12 days of Christmas equals the sum of the squares of all even numbers up to and including twelve! This equals 4 + 16 + 36 + 64 + 100 + 144 = 364.

So if we returned one gift per day starting the day after Christmas, we'd be all out of gifts by the following Christmas Eve! (The idea for this puzzle originated with Sidney Kravitz.)

74. SIX-POINT LANDING

One solution is given below. Note that it is impossible to add a tenth segment without forming at least one triangle.

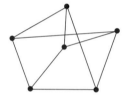

75. CUT AND PASTE

The key step is to notice that the length of a side of the square must equal the square root of 5. (See the diagram on the next page.) To create a side of length the square root of five, simply draw a line starting at the lower left corner of the original diagram and continuing until it meets up with the top of the diagram one little square over. That line forms the piece labeled A, which is a right triangle. The hypotenuse of A equals the square root of five by the Pythagorean theorem. Then draw the other two lines and reassemble the pieces as in the diagram at the right. The result is a perfect square.

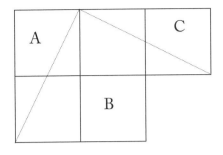
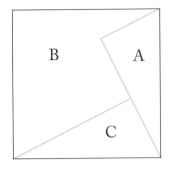

76. FRACTIONS OF THE WHOLE

$\frac{1}{4} + \frac{1}{72} = \frac{19}{72}$

77. STRANGE RELATIONS

The missing number is 5.

The rule that connects the top and bottom rows is that the bottom row gives the number of letters in the number above it. "Twelve" has six letters, "six" has three letters, and "three" has five letters.

78. DIGITAL PUBLISHING

The way to approach the problem is to group the pages that have the same number of digits. Pages 1 through 9 account for nine digits. Pages 10 through 99 account for 180 digits. That leaves 111 digits (300 − 189) for the three-digit numbers. Now 111 ÷ 3 = 37, so the book must have an additional 37 pages, beginning with page 100. That means the total number of pages in the book is 136.

79. LETTER PERFECT

C must equal 1 because $A + B$ plus the carryover cannot add to a number larger than 19. Since $A + B = A$ and B isn't zero, we know that B plus the carryover must equal 10. The maximum carryover possible when adding two digits is 1, thus $B = 9$. It follows that $A = 2$. The sum looks like this:

$$
\begin{array}{r}
2\ 9 \\
+\ 9\ 2 \\
\hline
1\ 2\ 1
\end{array}
$$

80. CONNECT THE DOTS

Ten lines will do the trick, as in the following diagram:

81. MINDING YOUR P'S AND Q'S

Note that $6249 + 3751 = 10{,}000$. Also, note that $6249 - 3751$ has the same value as $26{,}249 - 23{,}751$ because they each end in the same four digits. We'll use both of these ideas.

Add the original equations.

$10{,}000p + 10{,}000q = 50{,}000$.

Dividing by 10,000, we have $p + q = 5$.

Subtract the original equations.

$6249(p - q) - 3751(p - q) = 26{,}249 - 23{,}751$

$(6249 - 3751)(p - q) = 26{,}249 - 23{,}751$

The numerical values are the same on each side.

Canceling give $p - q = 1$.

Since $p + q = 5$ and $p - q = 1$, it is simple to solve and get $p = 3$ and $q = 2$.

82. MAKING THE GRADE

In order for everything to work out in whole numbers, we must have 24 students in the class, because 24 is the only common multiple of 3, 4, 6, and 8 that is less than 30. Adding the fractions gives $\frac{1}{3} + \frac{1}{4} + \frac{1}{6} + \frac{1}{8} = \frac{(8+6+4+3)}{24} = \frac{21}{24}$, so 21 students have been accounted for with grades "B" or lower. That means 3 students must have received an "A" on the test.

83. FEEDING THE SQUARE ROWS

Here are the six rows:

> 1, 24, 120
> 2, 23, 98
> 3, 22, 78
> 4, 21, 60
> 5, 20, 44
> 6, 19, 30

To obtain the numbers in the third column, note that the differences of the numbers in the first and second columns—from the bottom, 13, 15, 17, 19, 21, and 23—are precisely the successive differences between the consecutive squares 36, 49, 64, 81, 100, 121, and 144. So if we place 30 at the bottom of the third column, we have 6 + 30 = 36, a perfect square, and automatically 19 + 30 = 36 + 13 = 49, the next perfect square. Continuing in this fashion, we see that the sum of the first and third columns (from the bottom) equals six squared through eleven squared, while the sum of the second and third columns (again, from the bottom) equals seven squared through twelve squared.

84. CHECKER PIECES

The two pieces below are identical in shape. If you slide the lower piece upward, it will join with the upper piece to form precisely the original checkerboard piece.

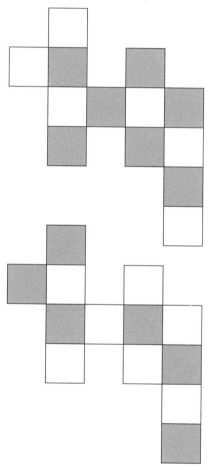

85. HOOK AND LADDER

The ladder slid out 8 feet. The ladder is 25 feet long, the distance down the wall is 24 feet, and, by using the

Pythagorean theorem, we can calculate that the distance along the ground is 7 feet. That is, the ladder originally formed a 7–24–25 triangle. After the slide, the ladder is still 25 feet long, the distance down the wall is 20 feet, and, by using the Pythagorean theorem, we can calculate that the distance along the ground is 15 feet. The ladder now forms a 15–20–25 triangle. Since the distance along the ground went from 7 feet to 15 feet, the bottom of the ladder slid out 8 feet.

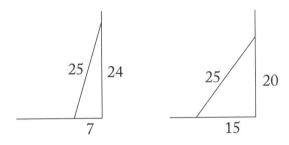

86. CUBIC'S RUBE

Both the top diagram and the bottom one can be bent to form a cube. The middle one cannot be folded to form a cube, no matter how hard you try.

87. AGENT 99

$9 + 8 + 7 + 65 + 4 + 3 + 2 + 1 = 99$
$9 + 8 + 7 + 6 + 5 + 43 + 21 = 99$

88. ONE, TWO, THREE, FOUR

Label the boxes A, B, C, and D as shown below. Then A and D have one ×, A and B have two ×'s, C and D have three ×'s, while B and C have four ×'s.

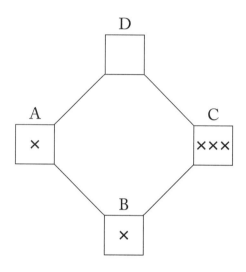

89. TRICKY COMBINATIONS

Here are my answers, which may differ from yours:

$20 = (6 + 4) \times (3 - 1)$
$21 = 31 - 6 - 4$
$22 = (6 \times 4) + 1 - 3$
$23 = (6 \times 3) + 4 + 1$
$24 = 3 \times (14 - 6)$
$25 = 4 \times (6 + 1) - 3$

$26 = (6 \times 4) + 3 - 1$
$27 = 6 \times (4 + 1) - 3$
$28 = (6 \times 4) + 3 + 1$
$29 = 31 - 6 + 4$
$30 = (6 + 4) \times (3 \times 1)$

90. CUTTING CORNERS

Cut the figure as shown.

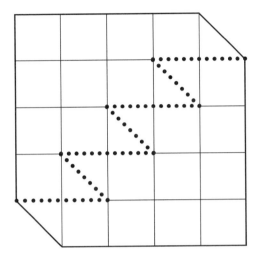

The two pieces can be put together to form the 4 × 6 rectangle as follows:

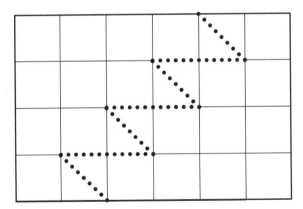

91. AS THE CROW FLIES

The picture must have looked something like the diagram below. Thelma and Louise were standing at the intersection at the top left. Alfredo's was eight blocks down and one block over, for a total of nine blocks. Bernardo's was four blocks down and seven blocks over, for a total of 11 blocks. However, note that because $8^2 + 1^2 = 7^2 + 4^2 = 65$, the two restaurants were exactly the same distance away, as the crow flies.

This solution isn't unique: For example, going 11 blocks down and 2 over versus 10 blocks down and 5 over would satisfy the same mathematical conditions as the answer above. However, maybe we can assume that Thelma and Louise were too tired to even consider walking 15 blocks!

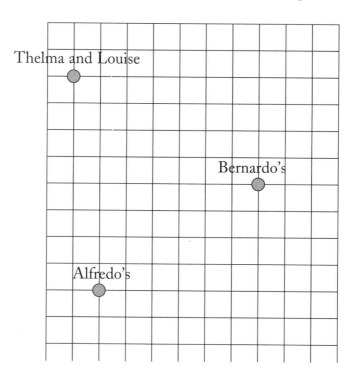

92. COUNTIN' IN THE RAIN

The vacation was 20 days long. We can have rainy mornings followed by clear afternoons, clear mornings followed by rainy afternoons, or clear mornings followed by clear afternoons. We just can't have any totally rainy days.

Let M represent the number of rainy mornings. Then the total number of mornings in the trip was 12 + M. Let A represent the number of rainy afternoons. The total number of afternoons was 13 + A. Since the number of mornings in the trip is equal to the number of afternoons in the trip, we have 12 + M = 13 + A. Rearranging, M − A = 1.

There are no totally rainy days, and it rained on 15 days, so M + A = 15. Solving the system of equations, we have M = 8 and A = 7. The vacation was 12 + 8 = 20 days long.

93. REVERSAL OF FORTUNE

$24 + 3 = 27$
$24 \times 3 = 72$

$47 + 2 = 49$
$47 \times 2 = 94$

94. ORDER IN THE COURTS

Sorry, but it's a trick question. Only three courts will fit, because the regulations state that any tennis courts built in the upper two-thirds of the United States must run north-south! Below is one possible layout for the three courts:

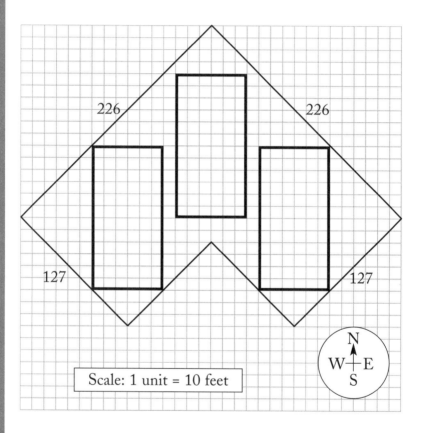

226   226

127   127

Scale: 1 unit = 10 feet

N
W+E
S

95. COLORING BOXES

Call the first player A and the second player B. Number the grid as follows:

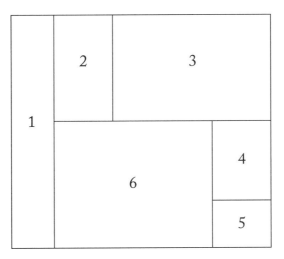

Here are all of the cases. On the second move, player B always chooses the color opposite from A's color. All of the other color choices are restricted by the rules, unless otherwise indicated.

A1, B5, A2, B4
A1, B5, A3 (either color),
   B2 or B4 (whichever is
   legal)
A1, B5, A4, B3
A2, B4, A1, B5
A2, B4, A5, B1
A3, B6, A1, B5
A3, B6, A5, B1

A4, B2, A1, B5
A4, B2, A5, B1
A5, B1, A2, B4
A5, B1, A3 (either color),
   B2 or B4 (whichever is
   legal)
A5, B1, A4, B3
A6, B3, A1, B5
A6, B3, A5, B1

96. EASIER BY THE DOZEN

Start by cross-multiplying, and then build a factoring on the left side as in question #59:

$XY = 10X + 10Y$

$XY - 10X - 10Y = 0$

$XY - 10X - 10Y + 100 = 100$

$(X - 10)(Y - 10) = 100$

The values in parentheses represent two whole numbers that multiply to give 100. The possibilities are (1,100), (2,50), (4,25), (5,20), (10,10), (20,5), (25,4), (50,2), (100,1).

Adding 10 to the numbers in each pair give the values for X and Y, which are the solutions to the original equation. These values are (11,110), (12,60), (14,35), (15,30), (20,20), (30,15), (35,14), (60,12), (110,11).

97. A REGAL CHALLENGE

You can move from R E G A L to G L A R E in an odd number of moves as follows:

	R	E	G	A	L
1	R	E	G	L	A
2	R	G	E	L	A
3	R	G	L	E	A
4	R	G	L	A	E
5	G	R	L	A	E
6	G	L	R	A	E
7	G	L	A	R	E

Note that even though LARGE and LAGER are words that can be formed using the same letters, you can't get from REGAL to either of these words in an odd number of moves.

98. CIVIL DISOBEDIENCE

The sum of those 13 numbers must be even. Note that C, which equals 100, is one of those numbers. Of the remaining 12 numbers, six start with C and six are these same numbers with the C removed. But adding any such pair of numbers (one with a C in front and one with the C removed) will give an even sum. Therefore the sum of all six pairs plus 100 (= C) must also be even. For the record, the 13 numbers are given below. They sum to 836.

$$
\begin{array}{llll}
C & = 100 & & \\
CI & = 101 & I & = 1 \\
CII & = 102 & II & = 2 \\
CIV & = 104 & IV & = 4 \\
CV & = 105 & V & = 5 \\
CVI & = 106 & VI & = 6 \\
CL & = 150 & L & = 50
\end{array}
$$

99. WHEN WE MEET AGAIN

The next meeting is in $12/11$ of an hour. Since both hands are moving at constant rates, they meet at regular intervals. The hands of a clock don't cross each other between 12 and 1 or between 11 and 12, but they do meet at 12. So in any 12-hour stretch, the hands meet exactly 11 times. If the hands meet regularly 11 times in any 12-hour stretch, then they meet every $12/11$ of an hour. So the next meeting after noon is $12/11$ of an hour later, or at 1:05:27$3/11$.

100. THREE'S COMPANY

$9 = 3^3 \div 3$

$9 = \sqrt{(3^3 \times 3)}$ or $9 = 3\sqrt{(3 \times 3)}$

$9 = 3^{3!} - (3!)!$

93

Index

Answer page numbers are in *italics*.

About the Author

DERRICK NIEDERMAN is the author of *Number Freak*, *The Puzzler's Dilemma*, and several volumes of math puzzles and brainteasers. He has also invented a variety of games and puzzles, including 36 Cube and PathWords. He lives in Charleston, South Carolina, and teaches mathematics at the College of Charleston.